O
PLANET

written by Priscilla Hannaford
illustrated by Studio Boni/Galante
and John Dillow

Contents

A Planet in Space

Our planet, the Earth, is one of nine planets that travel round the sun. It takes a year for the Earth to **orbit** the sun.

The planets are all very different from one another. Some, like the Earth, are made of rocks, while others are nearly all **gas**. Pluto is extremely cold, while Venus is too hot for anyone to live there. Some planets have rings and many moons. The Earth is the third planet from the sun and has one moon.

The planet Neptune is surrounded by a set of dark rings.

The Solar System

The Solar System is the name given to the sun, the nine planets and millions of **asteroids** and **comets** that orbit the sun.

The planets take different amounts of time to circle the sun. Pluto, for example, the planet furthest from the sun, takes

Comets have heads made of rock and ice and long bright tails made of gas and icy dust. Asteroids are tiny rocky planets, and most of these are between Mars and Jupiter.

Jupiter

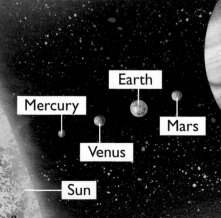

Mercury

Earth

Mars

Venus

Sun

248 Earth years to complete one trip. That means if you lived on Pluto, you would have to wait 248 Earth years for your first birthday!

Pluto

Uranus

Neptune

Saturn

The sun is a star just like all the other stars you see twinkling in the sky at night. It looks much bigger and brighter to us, however, because it is the nearest star to our planet.

The Earth

From space the Earth looks surprisingly blue. That's because nearly three quarters of our planet is covered with water. The Earth is the only planet known to have the perfect conditions for living things to grow, because there is plenty of water and air.

Astronauts are the only people who have ever seen the Earth as a whole planet like this. You have to be out in space to see this view.

Inside the Earth

The Earth has a number of layers, like an apple. It has a skin, called the crust, which is made of rock. The fleshy part is called the mantle and is made of hot, melted rock. The outer and inner cores are made of metal – mostly iron.

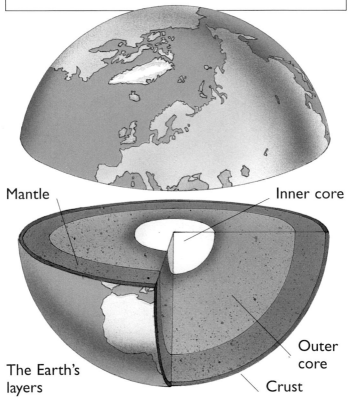

Mantle

Inner core

The Earth's layers

Outer core

Crust

Volcanoes and Rocks

Volcanoes are formed when hot melted rock called lava gushes up from inside the Earth and breaks through a weak spot. Lava is red hot at first but cools and hardens into a grey or black rock. Volcanoes that erupt regularly are called **active**. Volcanoes that show few signs of life are called **dormant**.

Some volcanoes erupt suddenly, without any warning at all. Others produce gentle puffs of smoke every few minutes. **Extinct** volcanoes haven't erupted in thousands of years.

The Earth is made of all different kinds of rocks. Some, like basalt, are formed by volcanoes. Others, like sandstone, are formed from grains of sand, mud or shells pressed together.

Sandstone

Remains of animals that lived long ago – called fossils – can often be found in sandstone.

Basalt

Basalt is usually black or grey and is made of tiny **mineral** crystals.

Marble

Marble is formed by being squeezed and heated.

The Ocean

Millions of years ago the steam which surrounded the Earth cooled and became water. Huge areas of salty water are usually called oceans, although some are called seas. A number of very large inland lakes are also called seas.

The seas are a treasure house. In some places, deep beneath the sea floor, oil and gas have been found.

Wells are drilled into the seabed to pump up the precious resources of oil and gas.

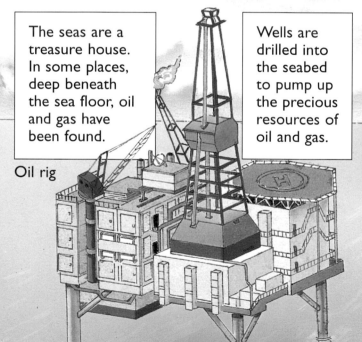

Oil rig

Long lost treasure

Divers search for
treasure from
sunken shipwrecks.
Many ships which
sank in bygone
days have still not
been found.

Treasure that has
been found ranges
from gold bars to
ancient porcelain.

Underwater exploration

Underwater
craft are used
to find wrecks
in deep water.

13

Mountains

As you climb a high mountain, the weather becomes colder and colder, and the air becomes thinner the higher you go.

The highest mountain in the world is Mount Everest in the Himalayas, in Asia. The first climbers to reach the summit were Tenzing Norgay and Edmund Hillary in 1953.

Mountains are dangerous places because the weather can change very quickly. There is also the danger of **avalanches**.

Mountain animals

Some animals like the mountain lion, mountain goat and yak – a kind of long haired cow – are specially adapted to living high up. They feel at home on steep rocky ledges, and can survive in extreme cold and windy weather.

Deserts

Deserts are either extremely hot or extremely cold, and only have a tiny amount of rain over a whole year. There are few plants and animals in the desert because it is difficult for them to survive without rainwater.

Desert plants like cacti have sharp spikes instead of leaves to prevent them from losing precious water during the blazing heat of the day.

Plants called succulents also grow in deserts. They can store water in their thick fleshy leaves. They live for well over 100 years.

During the day, deserts are extremely hot. People who live in the desert have to make sure that they have enough shade, food and water.

Rainforests

Rainforests grow near the Equator, where it is always very hot and very wet and there are no **seasons**. Rainforest trees have very tall, thin trunks. The leaves and branches of the treetops merge together forming a forest roof.

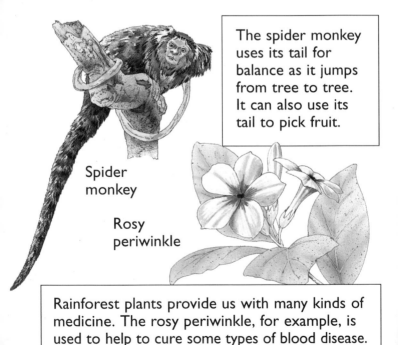

The spider monkey uses its tail for balance as it jumps from tree to tree. It can also use its tail to pick fruit.

Spider monkey

Rosy periwinkle

Rainforest plants provide us with many kinds of medicine. The rosy periwinkle, for example, is used to help to cure some types of blood disease.

Many animals live in this top layer, where it is light and warm with plenty of rainwater and, in turn, food.

Rainforest trees make an excellent playground for monkeys and apes. The chimpanzee uses its arms to swing between branches. Families of gorillas make cosy homes on the forest floor.

Other Kinds of Forests

In parts of the Earth where there are seasons, many trees are deciduous, so they shed their leaves in autumn.

Other kinds of forests are **evergreen**. These tend to grow in colder climates. Most evergreen trees have needles rather than leaves.

Oak leaves

Acorns

A lot of evergreen trees produce cones. They ripen in the summer, then open up and let the seeds drop out. Squirrels and some birds like the seeds inside the cones.

Pine needles

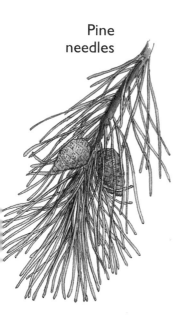

Cold Polar Caps

The areas around the North Pole and the South Pole are the coldest places on Earth. Here the ice never melts and no trees can grow because it is too cold. In summer, the sun never sets, and in winter, the sun never rises. The land is dark for months on end.

In the summer tiny flowering plants grow close to the ground so that the strong winds won't damage the blooms.

In spite of the bitter cold, howling winds and blizzards, an amazing variety of animals do live in polar regions.

Penguins have a thick covering of water-resistant feathers.

Penguins

The fur of Arctic foxes becomes white during the winter so that they blend in more with the snowy background.

Arctic foxes

Snowshoe hares

Huge, wide feet help to prevent snowshoe hares from sinking into soft snow.

Weather

The Earth is surrounded by an invisible layer of air called the **atmosphere**. The air is heated by the sun, which makes it move about, and we feel this movement as wind. The moisture in air and the motion of air create all the different kinds of weather – from snowy blizzards to gentle rainstorms.

The world's winds

Wind is air that is moving from one place to another. As air is heated by the sun, it rises, then colder air moves in to take its place.

Lightning is an extremely hot bolt of electricity that forms in a thundercloud. The sound of a clap of thunder always follows a flash of lightning.

Hurricanes are violent, swirling funnels of warm, wet air. They are most common in hot countries that lie near the sea and they can cause a great deal of damage.

Snowflakes are formed from ice crystals that join together in very cold clouds. Each and every snowflake that falls is unique.

The Atmosphere

The Earth's atmosphere is made of several layers. The **ozone layer** helps to protect us from some of the sun's more harmful rays.

Satellites orbit the Earth at heights of 1,000 kilometres above the Earth.

Satellite

A space shuttle is launched by a rocket high into the atmosphere.

Space shuttle

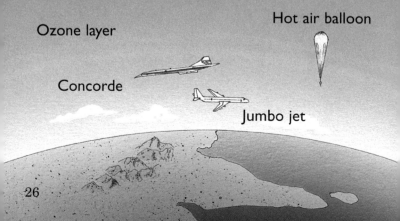

Hot air balloon

Ozone layer

Concorde

Jumbo jet

The sun is extremely hot and gives out lots of **energy**. Some of this energy warms the Earth and some is reflected back into space by clouds.

Pollution that people create is changing the mixture and balance of gases in the Earth's atmosphere. Some of these gases, especially carbon dioxide, are trapping heat from the sun, like glass in a greenhouse.

Scientists think this 'greenhouse effect' is making the Earth warmer.

Caring for Our Planet

The Earth is a fragile planet. Animals, plants, air, mountains, forests and seas are all dependent upon one another, so we must not upset the balance of nature.

In some countries wood is used to keep warm and to cook. But if trees are cut down, they must be replaced.

There are many
plants that are
endangered because
they have been
picked or dug up,
without others being
replanted. There are also many animals that
are endangered or have become extinct.

Nature reserves are special areas that have
been set aside to protect wildlife and rare
kinds of wild plants.

Glossary

Active A volcano that has erupted at least once in the last 10,000 years.

Asteroids Very small planets, mostly between Mars and Jupiter.

Atmosphere The mixture of gases that surrounds the Earth.

Avalanches Large masses of snow and ice crashing down the sides of mountains.

Comets Objects with bright heads and long tails that travel round the sun in a very long thin path.

Dormant Volcanoes that have not erupted recently.

Energy The power to do work.

Evergreen A tree or bush that does not lose its leaves in winter.

Extinct A volcano that is thought to be dead.

Gas A material like air, which is not solid or liquid.

Mineral A crystal which makes up rocks. It is formed naturally in the earth.

Orbit The path an object takes as it revolves round a planet or star.

Ozone layer A layer of gas in the atmosphere which protects the Earth from the harmful rays of the sun.

Pollution To make sea, land or air dirty and unfit for use.

Seasons Periods of time each year (spring, summer, autumn, winter), marked by different weather conditions and hours of daylight.